About the book

This book is a collection of 40 lyrics or poems. Mostly are love poems or love lyrics. This is the inspiration shared by the author and made shareable to you. Please feel free to choose and make music to any or all of the lyrics. This won't take too much of your time. Let us share love. Some are sad songs; some are happy ones. Some are about feelings. Some are about life. Some are mere feelings. Each word, each note has meaning and life.

This book is dedicated to my relatives: Tiya Wena, Tiya Tali, Tiya Myla, Tiya Marina, Tiya Tapin, Tiya Ana, Tiyo Jose, Tiyo Toni.

About the Author

Ismael Tabuñar Fortunado

I am an Engineer, an author, an inventor, a poet, a lyricist, a novelist, a fellow candidate, a theorist, journal reviewer, writer and a researcher. I am from Caloocan City, Philippines. I am an author of 20 books and three book chapters. I have four inventions. I am the author of 35 researches. I wrote over 600 poems. I am currently working on different areas of science, arts and theology. I was employed by WNS World Choice Travel as Operations Associate, UCONNECTS as Sales Agent, Bestank Manufacturing Corporation as Customer Care Agent, Maynilad Water Services, Inc. as Project employee, St. Joseph College of Novaliches, Inc. as teacher and Philippine Long Distance Telephone as Assistant Project Engineer. I joined few notable societies: National Research Council of the Philippines, Filipino Inventors Society and Philippine National Philosophical Research Society.

He invented one of the best perpetual calendar.
He solved the collatz conjecture. Only the tail has a cycle. Division is repeated subtraction. The (an) IDs or identifications are (could be) infinite.
He solved the fermat's last theorem using difference analysis or gap analysis.
He solved the beal conjecture using difference analysis or gap analysis.
He wrote Human Kingdom, separating man from animals.
And a lot more.

Ain't it funny

Ain't it funny to see the pets
Minding their own thing.
See how they play
All over and over again.

Ain't it funny how you lie
Like there is no tomorrow.
No wonder why
You brighten up my day.

Ain't it funny how we see
The beauty of this world.
The wonderful things.
Ain't it funny, is it?

Ain't it funny, you are beside me.
Not minding the hours.
Not minding the time.
How can you lie?

Love still matters.
Keep some to you heart.
Wait till the leaves fall down.
Fall on our place, our favorite spot.

Learn to unwind.
Write some good lines.
Learn the tunes of the prophets.
Ain't it funny, is it?

Cold outside

I call your name everytime.
I see your face everywhere.
A picture of you everywhere.

You know it's cold outside
So bring me home to your heart.
How to get along so well?

You know this heart of mine
Is yours, forever yours.
All the walls are gone.

All of the pairs are good.
You know what this brings.
I have been a fool all along.

Broken is what I am.
Giving all that I can say to you.
Bring me home, its cold outside.

It is cold outside.
Care to bring me a drink?
It is also dark here.

It is really cold outside.
Please bring me home to your heart.
How do you mend this broken heart?

Forever in a dream

You walked down the aisle
Holding white flowers.
Smiling so beautiful.
The best day of your life.

Wearing that white dress.
Wearing that finest smile.
Like the world would be better.
Like the world will be best.

Forever in a dream.
That is your finest dream
No one could take that away
Like it would be a sin.

How could I hold your hand
Close to my heart?
Everything in your memory
And our lips would touch.

It was all around.
Forever in a dream.
Like this is the last.
The last memory of you.

Good night, my dear one

The evening is good.
The evening is so inviting.
For us to sing some.
For us to be merry.

Don't close your eyes.
Open it widely.
Singing you this song.

This Sunday is so good.
This night is so merry.
Having to sleep.
It won't last yet you.

Cold is this night
If embraces are gone.
No need to worry.
Singing you this melody.

Oh the night is inviting.
Good night is for us.
Some singing, some dancing.
Making all the commotion.

Don't waste this time.
No nagging or gossiping.
This love is enduring.
Good night is this is.

Good night, my dear love.
Good night, my dear one.
Have a great one.
Have a good night.

Good Night

The sky is dark,
Clouds covering the sky.
There is no moon.
There is new moon.

This is a story of you.
How you took out my view.
I just thought
That I make you a home.

Good night, is there someone missing you?
Good night, hope your dreams come true.
Hope to see you smile each day.
Hope not to let go.

This promise will still be here.
Here where there is no more pains.
I have seen a perfect smile.
I have seen you cry.

It's a good night, a good dream.
Fight all the nightmares away.
Only good vibes I wish.
Wishing on a falling star.

Good night, it's nice to know you.
I guess this will be my last.
I have dreamt a lot.
Good night and good night.

Hi Hello How are you

Hi! Hello! How are you?
Do you miss me?
I miss you.

I was the first to smile.
It feels awkward but I.
I felt it with touch.
I know you are the one.

Hi! Hello! How are you?
Days passed, you and I.
Exchange greetings and messages
Like it were our last one.

Hi! Hello! Good moning.
What's for breakfast
My darling.

Its like the worlds closing in,
Already dreaming,
Already finding.

Hi! Hello! Good eveing.
How's your day?
How is everything?

Hi! Hello! My darling.
Take my time, don't haste it.
Hi! Hello! How are you?

Hiding the pain

Listening to the music
Not minding the heartache.
Tears are slowly falling.
Not missing a good try.

Hiding the pain is good.
Just to see you around.
You holding his hand.
Me praying on grounds.

Why does this heart ache?
You kissing him around.
Will this dream fade
Of being with you?

Am I just a friend
To get along with,
To have some fun with.
Oh it really aches.

All those memories bring pain.
I am hiding all the pain.
Why didn't I say to you?
That I really love you.

Hopeful

When I first saw you,
I was blue.
The day we met,
I felt something new.

Hoping I can see you each day.
There is nothing more I pray.
Where have you been?
It felt so long.

Looking at the time
As the winds pass by.
Seeing at the field.
The green all dry.

Sitting in the benches.
Singing some songs.
Hoping you can come.
Hoping you'll never go.

Hopeful is my love for you.
Hopeful to make good.
Hopeful I can say.
Hopeful that you'll stay.

How could this be?

You beside me seems so great but
How could this be?
How could this be that you brought smile to my face?
Love seems so great but
How could this be?

Your smile is so sweet.
It lingers in the back of my brain.
It touches my heart so earnestly.
It caresses my soul.
How could this be?

There is pain in my heart yet
You fill it up.
You fill it up with goodness.
How could this be?

I hope I could meet you even in my dream.
Tonight maybe or tomorrow when there is no rain.
A smile may do
If it is coming from the heart.

How could this be?
That now you are ignoring me?
Love is strange.
I could be lost.

I can't breathe.

You know what its like
To feel love, to feel pain.
You with someone else.
I can't breathe.

Its like pawn hanging by a thread.
Captured by an instant.
Captured by the heart.
You are my queen(king).

I can't breathe.
I slowly sink.
Sink in the ocean of your love.
I miss your touch.

The wind blown by the trees.
The leaves falling.
The trees crying.
I can't breathe.

You know what it feels like
Me beside you.
You stepping on me.
I can't breathe.

I was lost in the rain.

I was lost in the rain.
No more cure for this pain.
Everything seems the same.
Time has passed all again.

Fast as lightning,
No more frightening.
All I see is nothingness.
I wonder to be tall.

I was lost in the game.
The droplets drop so fast.
Then suddenly, it rains
Like the motion of the clouds.

Eager to meet you again
To see the sun again.
Look you in the eye
And wash your tears.

I was lost in the rain.
Trying to get a grasp
On the things you said to me
That you don't love me.

I'm just here

You walked away so sad.
Fighting so brave.
Fighting so hard.
Yet you lose your step.

Close to you.
Close to your heart.
Yesterday was a good day.
Tomorrow will be a good one.

I'm just here to hear you out.
Reminisce the times we had.
I'm just here, don't have to go.
You don't have to be alone.

I'm here, a loving one.
Don't have to go elsewhere.
I'll hold your hand.
I'll keep you warm.

I'm just here to keep.
Keeping the time with you.
Keeping you close
To keep you up.

I'm just here.
Don't have to say good bye.
A little time to be with you.
I'm just here to hold you close.

In the beginning

Was it love at first sight?
Was love enduring of the past?

In the beginning there was a warm day
Like the flowers smiling at you.
I have seen you nearby.

Wondering how can I meet you again?
How sweet is your smile.
In an open filed it shines.

How my life could have been
In an instant, in a dream?

In the beginning, there was you.
A sunshine of sweet dreams.

I thought life was unkind
With such smile, it's kind.

In the beginning, I'd go crazy.
Missing you in a memory
Like walking in a dream.

It hurts

It hurts to see you go.
You know I love you.
You choose passion or career.
It hurts.

It hurts to be with someone else.
You know I love you.
You choose to be alone.
It hurts.

It hurts that you are not ready.
You know I care.
You choose to fix yourself.
It hurts.

It hurts that it hurts more.
We are hurting each other
And this is not good.

It hurts that no one cares.
I wish to be lovable.
Even for a moment.
It hurts.

It hurts that you still care.
You know it's wrong.
We should not dare.
It hurts.

Last Time

Think of this moment.
Think of this crime.
Crime of loving you.
Was it ever right?

Could this be the last time we talk?
Could it be the last time you care?
I could have not let this pass.
Hindering how will this end?

Tell me what happened to you.
Share me your secrets and dreams.
I'm just a friend that loves you.
Will this be a last time?

Humbled by your word.
Could this be the last time?
The last time to see you.
The last time to care.

You never know how you meant to me.
You are the meaning, the meaning of my life.
Will this be the last time
Last time to see you?

Look

Hey there, young girl.
I wanna see your smile.
Hey there, young woman.
Let me shake your hand.

Look I have some things.
Will you buy some?
Will you take some with you?
Will you give me some time?

Pretty lady, look I have some gifts.
Care to see, care to buy.
I guess this is nonsense but
Full of meaning, full of sense.

Hey, care to see.
I'm just here.
I'm just around.
Take some time off.

How can I buy my life?
My life is going round and round.
Always in a hurry.
Always in a rush.

Look, the time is running.
Like the shortening of a candle.
Look someone is begging.
It is me for a life.

Loving

It is sweet to know the feeling.
Much sweeter to know the person.
It is in knowing that we learn.
It is in teaching that we unlearn.

How do we reach the clouds?
How do we smile too much?
All the time is ours.
Loving, loving, loving only you.

Loving, so sweet is this memory.
Taking all my senses.
That make me shiver and smile.
All I wonder is you.

Loving, all I care is this feeling.
Hoping this will last and nobody cares.
Help me, I am devoured.
I can't talk anymore, can't sleep too.

How long will this last?
My heart beats abruptly.
It says your name so loudly.
As I see you there noisily.

Loving, all I wonder is you.
I wonder if there is something in those smiles.
Deciphering this heart of mine.
Loving, loving, loving only you.

Melody

You are all over the place.
Your presence lingers.
Your passion speaks.
Something to remember.
Something to speak about.

You give me melody.
You give me another day.
You give me a heart.
You give me something to go by.
Your smile is a melody.

How the birds chirp.
How the clouds form.
How the sun shines.
How the leaves fall.
You give a melody to my heart.

You are my melody.
You are my song.
You give me something that I look for.
The world is sweet.
The world's lonely without your melody.

Moonlight

It's dark in the night.
Yet you are the moonlight.
It's cold in the dark.
You are with starbright.

I kept this feeling for a while.
I think about you each day.
Each day passes by like its nothing.
But with you, your smile.

It eases my soul like there is happiness.
The prophets' smile is with you.
The heart of a goddess.
The smile that pierces.

Moonlight, O where are you?
Hiding in the clouds
Or covered by them.
What phases do we miss?

Moonlight, it takes me there.
To the stars, the bright ones.
Signified by the brushes.
Is it time for me to sleep?

Once upon a time

Once upon a time.
Once upon a dream.
I wake up to good.
You are now beside me.

It is when you came.
Into my life, life is happy.
I never have known love.
But you came into my heart.

Once upon a time,
I dreamt of you.
You came into my life.
Never knowing this time.

Once upon a time,
We kiss each other.
I know you will come
And take my loneliness.

Once upon a time,
This pen touches the chords.
We sang too much.
We have the time of our lives.

One Thing

I know you are not me.
I wrote you a song.
Sometimes life is to be.
To be happy, one should.

You'll be married.
I hope not to be sick.
I'm happy that you'll be.
Happy and so this is.

Don't look back.
One thing, it may be three.
One thing, it may be free.
Smile, your day is great.

Writing you this song.
Something not me.
Singing you this song.
One thing I could give.

One thing, I know that's true.
Happy, I know you'll be.
Sadly, life is hard.
Dearly, life is there.

One thing to know is true.
Something, I know you.
Tomorrow you'll throw those kisses.
Sorrow the time won't misses.

Out of the blue

Out of the blue,
You held my hand.
Out of the blue,
You touched my heart.

You sang me a song.
You drive out my fears.
Out of the blue,
You mentioned my name.

When you came,
Life would be nicer.
Out of the blue,
You took out my blue.

I listened to you
To all the games you played.
Out of the blue,
You whispered so sweet.

It's because out of the blue,
My cold gone out away.
It's out of the blue,
A memory of you.

Paper

Take this paper.
Make a wish.
Take this paper.
Make a smile.

Hold your hand,
Sway it sweet.
Take this paper.
Call it hearts.

All I have is dust.
All I have will be lost.
Written in a paper
Is my love.

Have a letter.
Have a kiss.
Take this paper.
Make amends.

How I wonder.
How I fall.
Take this paper.
Hold them all.

This is me.
I have this paper.
I have this heart.
Will you take this paper?

Phantom

Ghost in you, scared to lose it all.
What do you seek?
Sleeping in the dark.

Walk to the light.
Singing with all might.
Ghosted are you.
Have you rolled a die.

Phantom O Phantom.
Where is your home?
Phantom O Phantom.
Where is your heart?

Singing you this song.
A lady ghosted me.
She too my heart away.
I have no more melody.

Ghost in you,
Where do I go?
I wish to be happy.
Phantom O phantom.

Rugged

Life is a rugged road.
Not a straight path.
Not a lighted highway.
Life will be forever life.

Take time to relax
Maybe on snow or mountain.
The distance seems to fair.
You may get weary.

Take time to unwind.
Not everything you do will people mind.
Hold on to something.
May be to a life.

Have somebody may be a friend.
A neighbor is good too.
A lover is there.
Have somebody to bless.

Rugged is this road.
A happy one may do.
Rugged is my love for you.
This is my road untaken.

Sad Song

Sad song, sad song.
Where is the music?
Sad song, sad song
The tears falling down the road.

Heartache, heartbreak.
My love's lost in a sad song.
True love, where are you?
Loving others is what we do.

Listening to this sad song.
Listening to its heartbeat.

Hold you till the end.
Let our minds collide.
Let us walk through this together.

Sad song, sad song.
Where is you smile?
Does it belong to someone else?
All you do is frown.

Is this the end?
Sad song, sad song.
All I hear is sad song.
All is left is this sad song.

Sight

You took my sight away.
With the beauty you hide.
You took my fears away.
Like a candle in the dark.

Sight is all gone.
A memory to remember.
All I see is you.
Sight is all yours.

Your smile is so bright.
Your look is so sweet.
How could I have fallen for you.
Seeing you from afar.

Could I only give sight?
Like a thanks to you.
You really took my sight.
With the beauty that you have.

What can I do?
I think I have fallen.
Like the leaves have fallen.
Because of the wind, shaken.

Please take me away with this misery.
Crawling like the king.
Sighting the fall so swift.
Contagious laugh that touches.

My sight, I give to you.
It was never a choice.
I have died once.
And this is all I have to give.

Stare

Hey there won't you stare?
Got a moment?
Won't you stare
Like eating my limbs?
Won't you dare?

There is no tomorrow.
How you wish.
You know that.
There is no forever.
Won't you stare?

Look at me as a man (woman).
I have feelings for you.
Feelings that should show.
Feelings that you should know.

Stare, love is a mystery.
Won't you stare on a window.
Full of symphony.
Stare, my love will show.

Each day, my love grows.
Won't you stare?
Each day, the love shows.
Why not stare?

Stargazing

How is your evening be?
Full of stars; full of dreams.
Wishing to catch some.
Wishing to be calm.

Look at the falling star.
Just like my falling heart.
Just break my heart in two.
Very crazy about you.

Everything served in platter.
We must be lying on the grass.
Counting each diamond aglow.
Seeing the tiny ones.

I just have to look at your face.
And see the star shines.
Beauty is evident.
Beauty is clear.

Stargazing all the time.
Stargazing all that's fun.
Sit beside me, lay beside me.
Stargazing all we want.

Strange

Talk to a stranger, talk to a friend.
Where does the story end?
Strange so it seems.
A loving story may mean.

Where does it begin?
Like the ink that does not cry.
Pulling out the cigar.
Throwing mighty the game.

Happiness is here or somewhere.
Destined to be happy.
Destined to be new.
All those treasures find their value.

How does it work, how does it feel?
To be untroubled water.
To be untroubled wine.
The end of winter is coming.

Call me crazy, call me fluke.
How did it matter to you?
Have felt its melody.
Strange is the question.

Have seen it all?
Have seen it dear?
The best will always be there.
We could have smiled.

Taken

Taken in a silence,
Taken in a dream.
How my life has changed.
With you by my side.

Dreaming to be taken.
Dreaming to be blessed.
How wonder time pass so fast.
We could be taken far away.

Taken in a memory.
Taken in a drift.
My life has changed
With you beside me.

This life is good.
Just seeing you always.
How could it be different?
A lasting memory.

My life is good.
It is because of you.
You have taken me.
Taken me wholeheartedly.

Three

Could I still count?
One, two and three.
I have given it my best.
How could we try another more?

All of the hearts are not waving.
If you could give me another try.
Hoping that we could have a family.
A happy one will do.

Three is a company.
Three makes my day complete.
Three makes the apple sweet.
Three is prolonging me.

I cannot make it on my own.
I have troubles on my own.
I cannot walk alone.
I want you to be with.

It scares me to be myself.
Not knowing what futures hold.
I want you to be there.
Like how we plant a three.

Untouched

Feelings that can't let go.
Seeing you forget the sorrow.
I know it and would not so.
How can this be?, I say.

Untouched, my love for you grows.
Untouched, I want a future with you.
Untouched, please pardon me.
Untouched, I am very sorry.

Feeling that won't leave.
Seeing you again makes me weep.
I know and won't let go.
All the troubles will go.

Seeing you amidst the pain.
Wondering why troubles came.
I know and happily.
Sick, I'm in tragedy.

Untouched, don't let go.
Does it matter if I love you so?
Untouched, a feeling so sweet.
Untouched, I hope for us to meet.

When

When will this pen touch the paper?
When will this song reach your soul?
When will the heart have its beat?
When will the girl know the cold?

I can hear you cry over here.
Over the dark, has taken its toll.
Why will I continue this wrong love?
Why will the scare has its feet?

No one is to blame, no one is to call.
Have you wondered it all?
When will this song be heard?
I have made you one good.

You are the only one.
You are too great.
When will there be treasure?
When will the instance be a call?

When will I see you?
When will I deeply truly know?
When will the sunshine be on me?
When is when, when is the day?

Whisper

You whisper in my ears,
The words I long to hear.
You whisper in my ears,
The love I should hear.

How could love be so great?
An undying one, a good one.
How could love be so good?
By your side always.

You whisper in my ears
That you will love me forever.
You say that love will shine
And that it will remain with us.

By your side, I will not part.
To be without you is a crime.
Like the ocean without water.
Like the river without sweetness.

Your voice weakens my soul.
The tender voice that calms me.
It is great to have you.
You are very sweet.

Thank you for your words.
The words I long to hear.
It keeps me closer to you.
I will never go away.

Without Caress

Songs come by
All sad goodbye.
Wish to sing you a song.
But all you have is goodbye.

This is my sad song.
Without caress.
A proper goodbye.
You left my life.

Longing to be with you.
Without caress.
But only you,
This is my sad song.

Help me with ease.
Help me with good thoughts.
For this is my sad song.
I only care about you.

Hoping to see you again.
Hoping to be in love.
Without caress.
For this is my sad song.

Without me

You took the fall
Like the waterfalls
Without me, you will still be great.
Without me, you will still be.

Why did this happen?
Like a broken glass.
Like a broken heart.
We hope to be stronger.

I appreciate your time.
I hope you do too.
You make my day great.
You make my day high.

Without me, you feel the rain.
Without me, I hope you are well.
No more rhymes, no more melodies
Will be left of me.

My life would not be complete.
Like the world collapse.
Like the vision won't unfold.
You have given me change.

Without me, you will still be whole.
Living in this memory.
Reflections on the waters.
Without me, but I do love you.

Write

I could have known you.
Everything was dark.
You gave a coin.
You gave me a seat.

It was the time I was four.
No longer in my dreams.
I am twice my age.
How could have been.

Thank you for the time.
I was confused.
You held my hand.
It is cold here.

Seems nothing is going good.
I have a melody.
I have some songs.
Longing in my dreams.

Everything will be fine.
How could it been.
I lost some touch.
I lost some golden lines.

You still love me.

I still see messages.
You still call.
You still wanna be a friend.
And that's not all.

You still love me.
I know you still care.
You still greet me
With the same high.

You still love me.
I know you do.
You give me chills.
You carry on.

No longer reasons could stop you.
It feels like ages that you love me.
You still love me.
You write on a note.

You still love me.
You still care.
In a memory.
You are still there.

You told me

You told me you are married
Yet you are not.
You told me you are happy
Yet you are sad.

Follow our goals.
A better future for us.
You told me your dreams.
I recall all of them.

You told me the sky is blue.
All blue because of me.
You told me you have no time.
No time for me, so sad.

I just wanna tell you this.
I just want to be with you.
Nothing more, nothing less.
You told me that, you told me this.

How can you tell me this?
You found a love.
A love so true.
You told me cries.

You told me a lot.
You told me so true.
How can't there be another you.
You told me, "I love you."

www.ingramcontent.com/pod-product-compliance
Lightning Source LLC
Chambersburg PA
CBHW051937150726
47999CB00006B/2255